Table of contents

Foreword - Alana Gracey

BACK TO BLACK

Collard green recipes

I am a black woman (essay)

Exhale

Soil

Ghettoblackbitch

BOYS MEN AND MOTHERHOOD

Black boys

Acceptance Letter

A Man

Gardens

Honorable Discharge

ADDICTION

No blame

I Get Migraines (essay)

Nephew, let me owe you one

Rhetorical

Church

HOMEGIRLS

Lil sister Malia

I asked 50 Women (essay)

The only

Back of the Line

Name Calling

Poem at 30

Ex friend

BLACK GIRL DOES A MATING DANCE

Car

You dating other people, right? (essay)

Unpacking

Call her sunshine

Magic

Candle Thrower

GET OFF'A ME

Forgivness

Idk what you were trying to bet out of me (essay)

Loud

Fair fight

Leaving

BETTER TO HAVE LOVED Spoons

Tis' better to have loved (essay)

Weeping Willow

Any memories

The native

Your books

Again with the memories

LATRODECTUS HESPERUS

Time again

Whoever said (essay)

Park at sundown

My grandma

Ol' Girl

It's Over

Dear Future Lover

Foreword

Having been friends with Nkenge for almost 10 years and having had numerous discussions about many of the relationship issues shared in this book, I am still amazed at how reading her thoughts have affected me. The power in her words is power indeed.

In *The Water Girl Drinks Before the Queen,* Nkenge tells my story. It's not my story word-for-word. It's not the timeframe of my story. It's not the details of my story—except it is. Each essay invites us into Nkenge's world. This timeline is uniquely hers, yet the poetry that follows every essay belongs to each of us. Every few lines, I experienced my life. I felt my own love and heartbreak. My own joy and confusion. My own feelings around falling in love and contemplating divorce. Several times I laughed out loud. I hollered. I snapped my fingers and spoke up in agreement. A couple of times I felt like I had been punched in the gut with a truth that I had been unable to articulate until I read it in her words. I mean, IT HURT! But it also gave me life. It even inspired haiku.

>the water
>
>girl drinks
>
>before the
>
>queen
>
>because
>
>she

accesses

the source

This is the realest thing you may read this year. Get into it.

BACK TO BLACK

Collard Green Recipes

Black mamas and grandmamas

Pass down what they can to they daughters

Weapons of survival

Tools they can use

Soft skin

Big eyes

And collard green recipes

We are around 10 years of age

When we begin our kitchen duties

Taught which foods soften ya' hands
during preparation Learn to
combine our efforts

Learn to listen out for the sound of big feet and tall tales

Men folk entering the house

Not the kitchen

But the house

Black mamas and grandmamas tell us

"He been working hard

That man

Fix him a plate nah girl"

Your ten year old brain wonders

How much food do you bring a man who never fills up

What a plate for an insatiable person look like

Yo' elders teach you portion control

Show you how to keep a second plate warming in the oven

'Case he want seconds

Don't he always want seconds

You begin yo' woman journey

Of fixing things for him

Keeping things warm

Keeping yo'self soft and busy

Quiet but relevant

Things you learn in this kitchen

Gon' come in handy

When you start yo' bedroom duties

Gotta make sure the food is just like he like it

Don't want him filling up elsewhere

It spoils if he don't want it, ya' know

You'll find nothing has meaning

'Til he give it some

You in the way girl

Gotta move round dis kitchen

On tip-toe

In heels

With grace

Get around all these
other women
somehow If you
can't make it in a
crowded kitchen
How you gon' make it
in a man's heart?

Black mamas and grandmamas

Pass down what they can to they daughters

Recipes

That call him home—or

Comfort you in his absence

Pots

That hold enough for a man who can't get enough

That hold just enough for you and the kids when he gone

That hold enough for the kids that are his but not yours

Black mamas and grandmamas

Teach they daughters and granddaughters

They way 'round a kitchen

A man's heart

Another woman's presence

Black mamas and grandmamas

Tell they daughters

"These recipes is 6 generations old,

Girl don't you go changing anything"

And we don't

We don't change a thing

It's been 6 generations since a damn thang changed

I am a black woman. An unambiguously-black, black woman. An end-of-autumn, leaf-falling-off-oak-tree, brown-skin, black woman. A, you-see-my-black-coming-fromdown-the-street-and-around-the-corner, black woman.

I was raised in the predominantly black city of Detroit where I got to live my life not as a black girl or a brown girl but as a *girl*. Growing up, I wasn't aware that there was any other type of girl. (And if there was another type of girl, she wasn't worth too many mentions.) In my family there were no comparisons of black women being better than, not as good as, or even equal to any other race of women because black women were the *only* women. The only definition of women. And we were not a collective generalization to be looked down upon. We were not one entity. We were individuals.

My father only allowed me to play with black dolls. He had subscriptions to *Ebony* and *Jet* magazines. I watched *A Different World* and learned how to do my own wet-sets so I could rock Whitley Gilbert's hairdo. (My favorite TV character honeymooned in the mist of the Rodney King riots!) My family, my community, and the media I consumed did for me what the rest of america does for white girls: surrounded me with many beautiful likenesses of myself. It allowed me to believe I was the alldeserving woman. All of the things I wanted to be when I grew up were illustrated by black women: a rich college girl, a wife, a mother. Hell, even Beauty of the Week. It left me feeling sure of myself. I was able to make it all the way to early adulthood before comparisons started to creep out of hell and into my ears. Though I use the word comparison, the act of comparing is fair and just in nature, so let me clarify: I made it all the way to early adulthood before I was exposed to black-woman "dragging" in the pursuit of white- girl praise.

In general, white-girl praise doesn't bother me much. It is almost always being committed by someone who I have no relationship with or interest in. Even more, it comes from people who I wouldn't give two seconds of my time to. (I usually think, "White girls, you can have this one. Thanks.") If my big nose, bigger lips, and/or actual or assumed loud, ghetto attitude keeps someone away, then praises to the Most High.

In my opinion, black people who are truly appreciative of their ancestors and aware of their own beauty are emotionally, spiritually, and physically attracted to black women. I believe that holding black women in the highest regard is an act of defiance, a continuation of the very defiance that ensures our survival. Loving black women devalues america's celebration of caucasoid beauty standards. If any black person is unable to see beauty in black women, they have purposefully disconnected from their ancestors, their history, and, ultimately, themselves.

With that said, I truly wish white-girl-praise was actually about desiring white girls, and not just another knife aimed at black women. I wish masculine lesbians and black men understood that you can like someone simply because you like them. But oh, no . . . That would be too easy—too much like right. Instead, they are liked for not being *us*.

In this matter, it is a common belief that I take issue with interracial relationships. Let me clear this up: I have issue with black women being degraded and verbally assaulted. I have witnessed several relationships where black women were in relationships with white masculine people. These black women didn't need to cut off a piece of themselves to enter those relationships. The women were still socially conscious and able to discuss their disgust with white supremacy and white privilege in front of their masculine partner, unedited. In the converse, every time I've encountered a black masculine person in a relationship with a white woman the relationship is rooted in the masculine person's hatred of black women. They haven't healed from that one time a black girl called them "lame" in middle school. Or the ever popular, "black women don't understand me." (It would seem that their love for craft beer and vintage cartoons requires an amount of understanding black women brains can't handle . . .)

Once I hosted a dinner party for six black, lesbian-identified women and we were candidly discussing women and race. One of the women in attendance who was going through a break-up proclaimed, "I'm tired of black women and y'all attitudes. I'm dating white women from now on." I continued checking on the food. I knew the woman who made that comment very well. We were close and I'd heard this "joke" before and knew she never made good on it. She enjoys getting a rise outta folks, and "a rise" she got. Another friend retorted, "Gon' head and date a white girl. Don't come running back when she has your pillowcase smelling like wet dog." This infuriated another dinner guest (who we all knew dated white women). She stood up and shouted, "If anybody has smelly-ass hair its black women; white women's hair smells like strawberries."

This is a woman who sported 24-inch locs—and at the time was engaged to a black woman. I stared, flabbergasted. Even if she had never dated a black woman, had she ever she lain on her mother's pillow as a sick child? Had she ever greased her sister's scalp or helped a friend take down cornrows? *Had she ever looked in a mirror?* When did she discard all of these experiences to make room for so much self-hatred and white-girl-praise?

america has always taught us white-girl-praise. Whistling at a white woman was punishable with death when black women were still property. This sad contrast of how black and white women are valued has been adopted by some black folks who have relationships with other black folks. They measure themselves by american standards, and consequently the black women they love.

Please understand, this ain't about interracial relationships. Also, this ain't even about white women. This is about black women. To be clear, I have no issue with any relationship that is built on love and *not* an attack on black women. I'm speaking on the experience of being a black woman who has dated black people *post* their interracial relationships. This is for black women who have had their blackness tokenized by black lovers. This is for black women who have waited at the arrival gates for lovers who return home (they always return home), who carry the baggage they return with, and are used for unpacking again and again. And again.

Exhale

"Would it be better if she were black?"
"No John it would be better if you were black" - Bernie, Waiting to Exhale -1995

I am not because I choose not to be

Feels a lot better than I am not because I cannot be

Yours is an infectious kinda love

Attacking my blood

My bones

Making it hard for me to walk

Reminding me to be mindful of my words

Making my words shape shift

Snatching words right outta my throat

Behaving
much like
slave
master Or
at least
overseer

Your love suggest I relax my hair

Warns me to avoid the sun

(Ain't I black enough already)

Just barely getting past the brown paper bag

At the door of your heart

I'm a more acceptable version of the completely undesirable

The best of the worst is no winner

No winner, no chance of winning

Your love reminds me that I'm pretty for a black girl

(Like wiping baby shit ain't as bad as wiping elephant shit But ain't it still….shit)

I know this watching movies

In the line at a grocery store

At work

In bookstores

I notice white women not noticing me

Do they know you've put us in competition

Did they volunteer

Did you tell them not to worry

This would be an easy win

Can I stop competing now

I'm tired and still black

Perhaps blacker than when met

Damn sure more aware of my blackness

My nothingness

We were together about 2 years before I asked you

If you have so much negative shit to say about black women

Why even date us

You said

"Well, I live in Detroit"

You said it like I'd asked you

Why yo' insurance was so high

My enemies

Have arrived in brown skin

Doing one hellava black face

Looking similar sounding familiar

Getting close enough to touch

Actually touching

Close enough to call me lover

Using their own blackness as part of the trickery

Hating me for being all the parts of themselves they run from

I'm black in motion

Black by popular demand

A spike lee joint in a mini skirt

Pulling you deep into the blackness you hate so much

But you chase so well

Soil

You've been calling me dirt the past 9 years

When I tried to wash up for you, you laughed and called me mud

I almost bit off my tongue trying to
twist my ain't into isn't You still ain't
hear me

You never heard my call

I'd assume you ain't hear me at all

'Cept you kept calling me too loud

You've been swallowing pumpkin pie and beer for dinner

For 9 years

I hear your stomach growling

Only white hands you craving are mine dipped in seasoned flour

You want in

Even if that means using the colored entrance

Now that it's time to build your house

You stop calling me dirt

Start calling me soil

Ghettoblackbitch

Do you think this my first time hearing it

You called me a loud, ghetto, black, bitch 3000 times in yo' mind Long before you found the courage to yell it at me in our latest argument

Long before you gave me side-eye for rapping along to Biggie in the car

Before I asked the waiter what the hell a fattoush salad was

Before I said "what up, doe"

Maybe it started when we stopped by my mothers

(You stayed in the car and hit the locks)

Upon my re-entry, you hit me with

"Wow, you really grew up here"

Ghettoblackbitch always rested somewhere in yo' mouth . . . waiting

Sometimes you folded it up, tucked it in back-handed statements

So tightly I almost didn't even hear it

"You sure do have a lot of books" or

"You don't act like other black girls" or

"Given your circumstances"

(Almost sound like compliments when said in the right tone)

When you sat cross-legged on my floor, soaking up my hood tales

I got to comfortable

Forgot that anything I say can and will be used against me

I wasn't careful

Allowed myself to become a point of reference in yo' urban studies class

Forgot that I am no Tigers game

You know

Just a reason to come to the city and buy cheap t-shirts

Allowed my bedroom to become a graffiti filled alley off Grand River

Didn't we both hear it dancing on your teeth

Before this argument

Before this day

This inevitable day

Where our experience with one another has worn thin

I shall make no apologies/accept no apologies

Feel everything but regret

Be every mad but upset

Be mad pretty

Mad smart

Mad witty

And I am prepared

For your slow-roasted insults

All their unoriginality

Curse me if you must

But remember

I am a hurricane

You are a meteorologist

Meaning the only time you'll ever be radical is when you chase me

Because you a storm-chaser

A name caller

An emotional gentrifier that steals anything black and broken

Like my heart, my spirit, this relationship

BOYS, MEN, AND MOTHERHOOD

Black Boys

In order for something to receive protection

Under the Endangered Species Protection Act

It must be endangered or threatened by at least one of the following factors

1. A decrease in natural habitat
2. Inadequate protection from man-made factors affecting its survival
3. Overutilization for scientific or educational purposes

    1 of 3 of these threats will save an elephant, a rhino, a damn spider

But Black boys natural habitat gets gentrified

Black boys be subject of Tuskegee experiments

Black boys learn to run with they hands up and heads low

Still ain't made no protection list

We've demanded no action

I'm raising a black boy

Sometimes I pull his clothes and search for the bullseye

Sometimes I make him practice holding his hands up

"Up baby, high real, high now, wiggle your fingers and scream unarmed"

I painted his inhaler red so it doesn't resemble a weapon

Cops and robbers have been replaced with cops and black boys

And you might be tempted to call this a war zone

May I remind you that in war

Both parties are armed

Both know what they are getting into

Both have eyes on the enemy

This is no war

This is hunting

Cops in camouflage

Black boys running free

Until they don't

How I wish you were the animal you get called

Instead of my son

I wish you were a rare tree

I would chain myself to you and demand

We honor your importance

I call my baby boy elephant

This is no cute pet name

This is me trying to convince the general public

He should not be cut down in his prime

This is me calling him anything but a black boy

Anything but a child of a woman named Nkenge

Don't black mamas have no mercy

No ride to an abortion clinic

No access to birth control

Why we keep having these black boys

Who die so young

They mamas buy caskets with baby shower gift cards

Black boys are dying before they school pictures come back

While they winter coats still big

We keep lying to em'

"Baby you gon' grow into that coat"

Black boys ain't growing into shit

Ain't filling nothing but cemeteries

Get funerals

Get hashtags

Get they pictures on t-shirts

Get everything but older

Black boys

Make the news

Make they 12-year-old cousins pallbearers

Make hoodies into political statements

Make they mamas

Do more
than just
consider
suicide Do
more than
consider
suicide

When all the black boys are gone

When we can only find their bones

Will we display them in glass cases

Or take those bones to museums

And continue to hang them

Acceptance Letter

Acceptance letter come in the mail

Mama smile/cry

Daughter run and tell everybody

Mama curse the part of herself that wishes

Her daughter wasn't smart enough to get into a university

Wishes this letter would have never found its way to her house

Mama stays up all night reading the acceptance letter

The school say they gon' cover 70%

Mama don't know what 30% of tuition is

But knows she ain't got it

See mamas who have had to sell pussy to make Christmas happen

Wonders what they'll have to sell to make 30% happen

But mama a hustler

I'm talking

Fish fry

Church fundraiser

Braiding hair

Pawned wedding ring

Moves in with Derrick

Yeah he cheat

And can't keep his hands to himself

But at least she ain't gotta pay half on shit

Fuck Derrick

Saves

Eats a vending machine lunch everyday

Saves

Owns one bra an entire year

Saves

No money for luxuries

Mama make that 30%

Takes daughter on a college tour

College gives mama a hoodie with school mascot on it

This hoodie cost mama 20,000

She gon' wear this motha-fucka everyday

Daughter switches her major

2 no 3 no 4 times

Comes home 3rd year of her 4 year journey

Notices mama 2 sizes smaller

Her ever present hoodie swallowing her

Notices Derrick staring…a lot

Daughter gets mama her own apartment

Gets homesick, gets lonely, gets pregnant

Fills mama's apartment with grief

Regret

And granddaughter

Now daughter going back to school

Just gon' take a year off to get settled

Gets 2 jobs

The first job is to pay the bills

The second job is to pay the babysitter

So she can work the first job

Daughter's night job

Is janitor at community college

She hears the half ass lectures

Prays her daughter never has to go to a wack-ass community college

Hopes that acceptance letter comes in the mail

Granddaughter spits up on mama's hoodie

She finally throws it away

Pushes it down deep into the receptacle

Next to her dreams

The dreams she had for her daughter

The dreams she dare not dream for her granddaughter

Mama still pulls out that acceptance letter and reads it

She sees where the school promised 70%

She remembers what she did for the 30

She laughs

'Cuz don't these colleges always manage to take us on a full ride

A Man

My son is 2

He sends me into a panic attack daily

I've spent a large part of mothering wondering

If I'm doing it right

A large part arguing with men

Who were raised by their grandma and mother

About how my marriage is a threat to his manhood

How two women can't raise no man

Let me say that again

I argue with men

Who were raised by two women

About how 2 women can't raise no man

When their logic is called out

They yell

Then threaten

Then leave

I'm sure these exchanges have affected my womanhood

My standards for men

How will this affect what I expect of him

How will he view women

And me

And himself

And today

My 2 year old tried to open a jar of candy

When it didn't open

He threw it on the ground, kicked it angrily

When anger didn't work

He threw it in the trash

Because if he can't have it

It must be worthless and disposable

So maybe he is already a man

Gardens

Last summer I made my son grow a garden

And I don't mean help me in mine

I mean, I made him grow his very own garden

A week after
we planted
the seeds He
ran outside
in boots

Trampled through the garden

Ruined the groves

Mixed the seeds

Fucked it up

Took a step back looked up at me and said

"Mommy why didn't you put a gate up?"

And I lost my shit

In that moment he was my father

His father

My brother

Every man who had ever ruined something

Been neglectful with his own creation

Then blamed the first woman he saw

The woman that loved him the most

And I realized how much he needed that garden

To understand how precious life is

How delicate he must be with it

And a counterweight to the fuckboyisms

He'll surely pick up along his journey to manhood

I made his ass replant that garden

First the sunflowers

To show him it's possible to tower over everyone around you And not be terrifying

Then the wildflowers

So he could see how much beauty happens

When he doesn't center himself

When he leaves something alone

Let him learn everything beautiful isn't a show for him

Last, the tomato's

He needs to know bulbs that don't bloom owe him nothing

Even if he brought it food

Gave it water

Offered it sunshine

Even if he is really, really nice to it

Let this garden teach him

His desires and anticipation are his own

Tomatoes owe you nothing

And let the knowledge of the tomato's autonomy

Make you value the tomatoes that choose to bloom more

When you realize tomatoes aren't unlimited

Aren't just growing for your consumption

At your will

Maybe you'll enjoy them with less haste

And more appreciation

Maybe if he grows this garden

He'll know that planting a seed is the easy part

Work hand-and-hand with a hoe

Respect the hoes contribution and talent

Learn to only kneel before things that bring forth life

God, Gardens, and Women

Work in rhythm with the earth

Learn that he is necessary but insignificant

Powerful and problematic by nature

Help him balance those inconsistencies with patience

Let this garden help him become a man that is always growing

Honorable Discharge

When I was a child

I thought my grandfather's name was

Billy Eugene Harris Honorable Discharge

He would say that shit like one word

Billyeugeneharrishonorabledischarge

Like he was reporting for duty

After retirement

Days he couldn't afford medicine

He'd buy a new flag and a bottle of E & J

I've diagnosed him

with PTSD 6 years

after his death

 Still faster than the

V.A.

He suffered from being an american

Who was expected to be murdered

Black southern vet

Learned to shoot deer

At 7

On his daddy's farm

Learned to be proud of his kills

Had so much blood on his hands he wouldn't pick babies up

Told me stories of the enemy

Kidnapping babies from orphanages

Strapping bombs to them

Leaving them in the middle of the road

'Cuz american soldiers were soft

Baby and soldier would blow up upon contact

His best friend loved babies

His best friend was soft

I've watched him pick up his homeboy in pieces

Again and again

E & J

PTSD

Make his homeboy appear on our kitchen floor

He lost hearing in one ear

I had to yell so he could hear me

But had to whisper so he wasn't triggered

Into picking his best friends pieces off the floor

This made conversation difficult

He talked to one side of his jaw

Showed me the gap in his mouth

Where the army removed a back tooth

So he could store a suicide capsule there

Dead men tell no tales

Not snitching is the only patriotic thing I do

I've noticed the memorials receive more attention than the veteran's center

Veterans have showed me you can indeed die twice

And best friends can blow up 1000 times

Veterans yell their names and their titles

From a grave they outran

To the promise makers they enlisted their trust to

Hoping somebody hear it

Somebody hear it

Some body . . . hear . . . it **ADDICTION**

No Blame

I want you to know

It wasn't all bad

In case I get upset at the bad parts

And tell you different

Even the bad has grown up

And made something of itself

Remember that summer we lived in the brownstone on Wildermere?

You sold every TV in the house

I remember

Living room (since we all had TVs in our rooms)

Your room (you never watched it anyway)

My brothers (he
needed to go outside
more) My room (you
wanted to be fair)

I got so bored that summer I started reading

Read anything I could find

Books

Newspapers

Ingredient list

Got really good at reading

Pretty fast too

By middle school

I could finish a Danielle Steele in 2 days

In high school

I read the entire reading requirement list in a week

Wrote all my papers

Got A's

Starting selling my classmates my old papers for $5

Writing their papers for $10

They had TVs

I had a hustle

Made this poverty marketable

Because of you

I ain't afraid of a good book

A little silence

An empty refrigerator

Or the dark

I ain't talking 'bout midnight darkness

I'm talking about the kind of darkness that only appears

In the black of not being able to pay yo' light bill- darkness

I wish a ghost would run up on me

Because of you I ain't afraid of shit

I am prepared for shit

Candles and canned food

Heat blanket in my purse

Been here before prepared

Been in the know

That this too shall pass

The good and the bad

It always moves along

Pass me, behind me, over me

But never through me

It wasn't all bad

And you should remember that

On days that regret creeps up on you

Like a roach to a box of cereal

Silent but aggressive

You are a survivor called many other names

Ain't you yo' mama's daughter

Yo' daughter's mama

Yo' grandson

Ain't never seen a bedroom without a TV

A refrigerator without his favorites

Or a night that threatened to hold tomorrow hostage

You are a teacher

In your victories and even more, your mistakes, mama

I get migraines often. Most days I lay down, or power through. I don't know if you can become addicted to over-the-counter drugs; I don't want to find out. I'm terribly afraid of becoming an addict.

After I delivered my babies, the hospital gave me morphine. I really, really enjoyed the morphine. It was goddamn magical. I enjoyed it so much I got nervous. Do you know how nervous you have to be to experience nervousness while on morphine?

I asked myself, "Is this what getting high feels like the first time? Is this what addicts are chasing?" I am terribly afraid of becoming an addict.

I don't drink. My father drinks enough for the both of us. His father too. I don't smoke. My mother smokes enough for the both of us. Her father too. I may be firstgeneration sober. I am at least first-generation sober as far back as we can trace. Every day still feels like 'one day at a time.' I am recovering from drug use. My mother's and her mother's. I am trying to hide the shaky hands caused by alcoholism. My father's and his father's.

Addiction, in my family, is like chitterlings during the holiday season. It is in the house, near the kids. We celebrate around it. Pretend not to notice—been sitting with it so long maybe we really don't notice it anymore. There are head shakers, and some weak protest: "Naw, I don't want none a dat." But every year, faithfully, at least one person gives in to curiosity: "Aye, cuz, lemme get just a lil' taste."

Nephew, Lemme Owe you One

I been up nights

Itching, scratching, digging

Touched all the layers

It's a bad day

When a black girl find her white meat

I been up days

That I swore was night

Eyes bloodshot and round

Eyes bigger than my head

Cain't keep my head up

Head down mo' appropriate anyway

I been sick

Off the very thing that make me well

Make me sick

I'm sick of this shit

Gotta get gotta get

Some more of that shit

To be well, to be sick To be at all

And dere go ma' main man Kev

Wonder if he remember I gave him ma' last dollar

My mama's necklace

Ma' body fa a night

I feel like he owe me one

He say we even

I say to 'em

"Aye, Nephew Kev, I need summin, I got chu soon's ma check come You know I'm good fa it . . .

Oh come on now, you can't spare a lil' shake?

I ain't trying to get high I'm just trying to get right"

He reminds me, "Dis ain't no damn loan office"

Fuck Kev, gon' rob his ass

He catch me, he kill me

He don't catch me, I get high

First win/win I seen in a while

He gotta go to sleep sometime

He ain't like me

I been up since 87'

Since my baby daddy said,

  "That weed ain't shit, lemme sprinkle something in there

You trying to get high right"

I watched the worm

The robot

The electric slide

The butterfly

The Harlem shake

Come and go

Come and go

I seen 27 Kevs

Come and go

Come and go

I den outlasted 'em all

Paid for hundreds of Jordans

Never owned a pair

My bidness bought
dey babies pampers
While my own
baby....

Well, I don't know what mine was doing

Best ask his grandma

Who says I'm dead to her

Or my son who only wishes I was dead

Or the 27th edition Kev

Who gon' kill me

Or die

And make room for Kev 28th edition

Who gon' scratch this itch

One way or another

Who owes me

A bag

The 90's

My son's whole childhood

Layers and layers of brown skin

Dis ain't no damn loan office

I won't a get a day back

But could you spare a lil so I could maybe get a night's sleep
Rhetorical

Do you find yourself Or leave

yourself in your high

Are you running toward or away . . .

Can you hear your children call you there

Do you even get high anymore

Are you just coping

Keeping the sick at bay

Does it behave like medicine at this point

Do yo' dealers wear white coats

Are you an ounce away from your prescription

Do you remember when you started

Does it hurt to remember

How many times have you quit

Is quitting even an option

What do you dream about

Are you high when you dream

Do you dream of getting high

Do you ever feel like an addict

Or is sober your uncomfortable

Would you believe me if I said I don't blame you?

Church

The church 3 blocks from my house gave free lunches to needy kids in the summer

They'd invite you to service

Wouldn't force you

But….highly suggested it

And you might even score an extra take-home lunch

If you stayed for service A cookie

if you sang

After so many free lunches

I thought it rude not to attend service

I learned

The Lord's Prayer

Going Up Yonder and

Hem of His Garment

Ate the second lunch on my walk home

Stashed the cookies and graham crackers for dinner

Or breakfast or a tea party with my dolls later

Where the dolls are talkative

I am not a girl who stashes food

We eat my graham crackers without saying grace

And for just a while I don't wonder where the next meal is coming from

HOMEGIRLS

Lil sister Malia

Malia,

When I was younger my father took me to his company picnic

I got a new dress and a warning

"Don't get in here and show your black ass"

Loosely translated

 "The attendees of this event are primarily white folks,

Do not behave in a manner that would prove a negative stereotype about blacks To be true"

That picnic was 2 hours long

2 hours too long

2 hours 1 hotdog and

A side of the worst potato salad in the world too long

I sat on a bench the whole time

Knew better than to get dirty

Mess up my hair or Be a child

Malia, I wasn't a child

I was a black girl

So even silent I was just a little too loud

Taking up too much space

Sitting on a bench

Trying to shrink into perfection

Eating just enough

So I don't appear rude

But not eating so much I draw

attention

So thankful it ended

I managed not to embarrass myself

My dad……a whole entire race

Malia your fathers picnic been 8 years long

You've been sitting on a bench

Keeping your hair neat for 8 years

Then you danced

Arms up

Hair flying

Dance Malia

Teach us how to stop shrinking

Show us that all it takes is a 90 pound black girl

Taking up a ton of space

Dancing like no one is watching . . . knowing everyone is

Black girls everywhere are with you

Relearning the dance moves they thought they'd

Scared, beat, threatened out of us

I asked 50 women, ages 19-65, to tell me the first messages they received as little girls about being friends with other little girls. Their general responses were:

> "They not gon' like you cuz you pretty."

> "All girls do is smile in your face and talk behind your back."

> "Never leave a friend around yo' man."

> "You came in this world alone and you gon' leave it alone."

> "YOU DON'T HAVE/NEED NO FUCKING FRIENDS!"

This is what we tell our daughters. This is what our mothers told us. This is what our grandmothers told them. We pass on this hand-me-down hatred like bowls of blackeyed peas on New Year's Day. As if it is a necessary life lesson on womanhood, "Wrap yo' hair up at night, capful of bleach in yo' bath, and never trust another woman."

I was taught that "bitches ain't shit" long before I was old enough to hear the unedited version of my favorite rap songs. This taught me to avoid pursing friendship with other women. And it taught me that if a woman didn't like me she had to be full of hate and jealousy. Even if we get older and reject these lessons, the subconscious doesn't forget so easily.

My homegirl, said "When folks get married, the groom's best friend is his childhood friend. The bride's maid-of-honor is a relative or girlfriend from college." In my experience (and that of many other women) there is no female equivalent of the ever-popular "bros before hoes." Girls start getting the message that women are jealous, sneaky, back-stabbing, boyfriend-fucking, disloyal, emotional creatures when they begin to socialize. So elementary school years, maybe three to five years old. We start telling girls they are becoming young women around the time they start developing breasts and/or having a period—typically around 11-16 years old. In other words, we spend about five years devaluing women, then we tell our daughters, "By the way, you're a woman!"

What I want to acknowledge is how hard it can be for women to befriend other women. How hard it is to cultivate and nurture those friendships when we weren't given the skills or allowed to desire those friendships. I want to acknowledge the homegirls who manage to have and to be homegirls despite all this. And to the homegirls who are experiencing the kind of lonely that can only be satisfied with friendship. Know this: You ain't alone in yo' lonely, sis.

The Only

I realize that I am the only black girl in the administration office

But your unrelenting need to compliment me is going to make your nose bleed

My syllabus doesn't say which textbook I need

(Which is the only reason I'm here)

RELAX

I am not attempting to Abby Fisher my way into your heart

Just give me my textbook number so I can get this masters

And live almost as good as a white man with a high school diploma

I am the only brown girl at the cocktail party

Except for the other brown girl

Hanging on to her husband's arm

Swinging strange fruit style

Who's been avoiding me like she's half afraid I'm gon' ask her to shuck and jive Half afraid we might actually be cousins

I'm showing way too much leg

Legs are covered in tattoos

Tattoos are on brown skin

(You can't decide which is more offensive)

I am the only black girl in the staff meeting

And no, I don't think we should have our next team-builder up north

News flash: leaves change color in the city too

That is a dumb fucking reason to travel

Anyway, what is your obsession with watching anything brown

Hang from a tree, detach from its roots, and die slowly

I am another black girl

Tired of leaving your events hungry and eye-fucked

Tired of explaining locs are not braids

Of repeating my name

Watching you stutter, choke on it and cough up

"Oh that's different, but beautiful"

As if I needed my name validated by a bitch called Hayden Dandelion Finklestein

All black girls have been the only black girl

Black girls aren't afforded shit like

Solidarity, a comfort zone, a jury of her peers

UNCOMFORTABLE be a part of our being

All brown girls have been lonely

Sitting up straight, arriving early, mindful of tone

Fighting stereotypes that box us in

Which perpetuates the stereotype that black girls like to fight

Can't win

But bet' not fucking lose

All black girls know

That she will die alone in a box

Black girl alone so much,
in a box so often Wonders
if she is already dead
somedays

At administration
offices and staff
meetings At cocktail
parties and in mirrors

Back of the Line
(for homegirls who have suffered appropriation and gentrification)

Black girls at the back of the line

Been back here so long

Starts to feel like home

We been back here so long we started dancing

Drumming

And twerking

Been back here so long we started a garden

Collard greens and carrots everywhere

Been back here so long we startin' ta get visitors

I think dey teachers

(Bring they notebooks and study us so)

Leaving wit' dey
hair in similar
fashion After filling
up on collards

And unsuccessful attempts at twerking

Dey think dey sent us to da back of da line

Ha! Na you should know enuff bout black girls by now

Ta know

We don't get sent no where

You should know us well enough by now

Ta know

If we there, whole groups of us

Dancing

Drumming

Growing

Means we wanna be there

We make homes where yall only see mess

Once you see we made homes you come

And make a mess

Call our rags and sticks reclaimed

Call our neighborhoods up and coming

Telling yo'selves you discovered

Our dances

Our drums

Our recipes

Our selves

It's impressive how you balance

Yo' envy and admiration

Black girl be a conundrum

Call us broken

And still collect the pieces

Whatever pieces you can get away with taking

Y'all ain't tired of taking yet?

Hairstyles

Dances

Recipes

Whole fucking people

Black girls at the back of the line

'Cuz we wait on
late comers
Show dem
hospitality

We been raised right

Taught well

Taught to never front
on those behind us
Never front on
ourselves

Maybe taught a little too well

'Bout forgiveness

Pushing forward Moving on

Our hearts

Big as our asses

Wide as our hips

Full as our lips

Always offering
a bit of

forgiveness
Even when folks
forget to ask
for it

Cuz black girls at the back of the line

Have each other

Have "my mama told" me wisdom

"My grandmother's recipe" medicine

"My cousin taught me" hustle

Have more than enough

Are more than enough

Can lead from anywhere

Especially the back of the line

Name Calling
(for homegirls who have loved fuckbois, and for Ciara Harris-Wilson)

They will call you too loud

Even in your silence

When you are only trying to protect yourself

By not summoning dragons

NOT saying his name

Last you called his name

He heard you

Came forth

Ran to you

Ran over you

He left you heavier

By way of child and heartbreak

Little boy and unclaimed baggage

Last time you called his name

He act like he couldn't even hear you

Maybe he didn't

Sometimes it's hard to hear love

Love be
talking in
hushed tones
While lust be
yelling

And he answered who he heard

Lust didn't yell louder cuz lust wanted him more

Lust yelled louder cuz love was in a choke hold

How did they twist your unspoken words

How did they forget all the times you called his name

In your lonely

Pregnant

Wanting

While you missed him or

Hated him or

Balanced the two

Would you prefer she call on her attackers

Celebrate her own heartache

Place welcome mats at the door of her recovery and burn candles upon his arrival

Would you prefer she forget her own name

Erase knowledge of self and only allow room for him

Let her have her tongue back

He's due no more

Due no calling

Singing

Saying of his name

What they call him before you anyway

Poem At 30
(for homegirls who have turned 30)

Tonight I am 30

I am as young as I will ever be

As old as I have ever been

Tonight I am 30

And I am so upset

About not moving to New York at eighteen

Not finding my voice sooner

Tonight I am 30

And I am so happy I took chances on love

On people

On love again

Tonight I am standing at the intersection

Of regret and possibility

I stand here in expensive shoes and cheap henna

Loving the tattoos they warned me I'd hate a decade ago

Accepting stretch marks that ain't going no where

Wondering if it's all downhill from here

Wondering where the time went

Writing this so I can read it on the eve of my 40_{th} birthday

As only women who have turned 30 can understand how young 20 is

I'm guessing I'll read this at 40 and say

Chiiiillllee

You wasn't nothin' but a baby

Ex Friend
(for homegirls who have had to break up with a homegirl)

I met her at pride 2002

And she was filled with it

She showed me how to use eyeliner to draw rainbows on my eyelids

Showed which bar had the good drinks

And which club had the bad girls

She was my homegirl

My, come ova uninvited Take

down my braids

Biiiitttcccchhh, catch dis Tea!

Homegirl

Was my homegirl because

Was is then

This is now

Now

Now I follow her online, this is how I know she's alive

Some version of her I don't care to interact with

My friend

Ex-friend

Tried to scream black power and gay pride at the same time

Nearly bit her tongue off

Which is still not as painful as jamming 3 types of oppression into her spine

Black

Gay

Woman

No good side of the bed to wake up on

No safe side of the street to walk on

No movement that would hold all 3 parts of you

You were pink elephant

Standing center of the room

They would acknowledge your

Tusk

Belly or

Tail

But never all 3 never at the same time

My friend

Ex-friend

Wanted to be discussed entirely

Wanted to be able to count her oppressors on one hand

Be black OR gay

Because OR is less oppressive than AND

Because it is so much easier to wipe off rainbow eyeshadow Than extract melanin

While being gay is not a choice

Pretending to be straight is

Passing ain't just for light-skinned negros

But keeps ex-gay girls safe just the same

I bumped into my friend

Ex-friend

At the African World Festival in 2015

She was rocking red, black, and green eyeshadow

Told me her makeup takes half the time now

She asked me

If I'd considered seeking help for my mental disease

I asked her

How is yo black so dark

That it keeps all the other colors prisoner

And shows you shadows of
who you once were That
it buries you in tradition

Serves you bowls of shit, covered in hot sauce

Do you buy yourself sage every 25th

And smudge yo pussy

You baptized yo heart, plucked out your offensive eye yet

She said

When you are ready you have my number

I love you anyway

I told her

I loved her anyway

Her anyway meant "in spite of"

My anyway meant

Anyway you are

However you be

Whatever they call you

I love you anyway

My friend

Ex-friend

Is a black girl

Surviving by any means necessary black girl

Tired of dodging bullets 3 ways black girl

'Fro framing her shame black girl

Blocking her peripheral no looking back black girl

I do hope its gets easier

I pray it gets better anyway

That both our existences become less offensive

Friend

Ex-friend

You do not offend me

In fact some days I miss you

I'm sure some days you miss you

Even the parts you buried in shallow graves

We know pride be a survivor

We know pride don't go down easily

Friend

Ex-friend

Living 3/5 human

Be bout as black as you can be

Black Girl Does a Mating Dance (dating)

Car—a short

Our first phone conversation, she talked about her car—a lot. She was so proud of her hard work paying off, by way of her dream car. Our first date she picked me up. The inside of the car was a complete mess. She must've noticed my shock. She explained, "I know I need to get it detailed; I've just been so busy."

I smiled and responded, "It's cool." And it was, as this would be our only date. I knew better than to fall for someone who left things they loved a mess, and collected things that they were too busy to cater to.

After all, this car demanded much less attention than I would.

She asked, "You are dating other people right?" It was a question that read like a statement and hung on the edge of our boundaries, waiting for my response. I needed to respond in a way that answered the question, honored the statement, and drew a line in the sand. My tongue betrayed me and pushed out, "No, no one else." She looked confused, shocked maybe. "Well," she continued, "without an agreement of monogamy I assume there is no expectation of it." I asked, "So you are dating other women." Another question in statement form. She replied, "I'm enjoying the company of beautiful, intelligent women and letting things progress naturally." I tried to relax my face in an effort to look cool, unbothered even. There was no cool way to say I thought we agreed to monogamy the first time we had sex. We were in a restaurant and I was determined to hold my shit together. I managed to smile and say, "Of course, I'm open to dating other people. I just haven't met anyone else I'm interested in." Now, why in the hell did I say that? As if she were not already arrogant enough, I had to tell her that the only person who I find interesting is enjoying the company of beautiful, intelligent women. Women? The English language is so fucking vague. Women could mean one other woman or ten other women. Women only implies more than one woman, more than me.

Our salads came. I watched her take a bite, chew, swallow. She was completely unaffected. I mimicked her motions. Bite, chew, swallow. I swear my salad had glass in it. But fuck it: if she's going to make me eat glass, I may as well satisfy my curiosity.

"When you say beautiful, intelligent women, how many women we talking?" I prepared myself for the answer. She offered, "Are we going to enjoy our time together or discuss what happens when we're apart?" This was one of those pivotal moments. We looked like two women having dinner, having a conversation, but we were dating. This was combat. She'd made her move. Now, I had to choose whether I'd sacrifice my rook or my pawn. One of us was going to walk away from this table without total possession of our own queendom.

I saw her again the next day; the next weekend; the next several months. Every time I dressed to see her I prepared for battle. War paint, body armor, attack strategies. I laughed at her jokes. Studied her likes, became them. Studied her dislikes, became the opposite. When I fucked her, I attempted to make her believe I was the muse that inspired the cyber-skin collection. For all my efforts I won small tokens. She silenced her phone when we were together. I met friends and was featured on social media. I stored these tokens like trophies. I felt like I monopolized most of her free time, therefore I was *winning*. Winning so much I don't remember when I lost interest. At some point I had stopped dating her and started dating the "beautiful, intelligent, women." Understand what I'm saying: I became so hyper focused on competing against my faceless, nameless competition that it was no longer about me and her.

I wouldn't say it was a waste of time, that year. I went to my first opera. I learned a lot about balancing in heels. Her mother taught me how to make bread pudding. I don't eat bread pudding, but I can make it if I ever wanted to. When I stopped competing, I took all of my medals: birthday gifts, life experience, her mama's recipes. I took all of my medals. If we were not a couple, it was not a break up just a finish line. I offered no closure, asked for none in return. Love can last a lifetime, competition only a moment. Dating is about learning yourself. Learning how to treat others and how to tell people to treat you.

These situations always end and I try to make the most of my exits. I leave as soon as the reflection is clear. Every person I've ever dated offered a reflection. Sometimes they were oceans I fell in. Sometimes they were compact mirrors that I lost and quickly replaced. Either way, I saw myself a little each time. The oceans taught me how to swim. The compact mirrors taught me there is no shortage on mirrors.

Unpacking

I've learned

That any woman desiring to date me

Has a special case of mommy issues

Enjoys S & M on Sundays

Celebrated her last birthday at a tattoo shop

Has hit an animal and kept driving

Loves her car more than her cousins

Is ambitious enough to leave

Is only half unpacked and ready to leave

Has left and

Will leave

Only argues with me to collect stories

To justify her leaving

Upon meeting her next temporary girlfriend

(Has already met her next temporary girlfriend)

Likes me because I'm easily distracted

Is counting on it to assist with her departure

Speaks in past tense about tomorrows plans

Arrives to our first date with memories of us

Arrives to our first date late, and still not ready

Reads the back cover of books in bookstores

Doesn't buy the book (never intended to)

Re-shelves it in the wrong section

Confuses the person that comes behind her

Compliments me in the same tone of obituaries

I attract women who are

Strong and capable Bored and

lazy

Who build homes

Only to discover they prefer lofts

Who buy lofts

And suddenly

Want a tent

Who are always remembering

What they forgot

And on their way to find it

Are attracted to my ugly parts

The parts that mirror themselves

Who love my scars

So much

They'll give me a brand new set

Are packing

Are in transit

Are waiting for me

And thanks to the women I've dated before them

I am already dressed for our date

In black

With a purse full of tools

That have never proven to be helpful

With a purse so full I have no room for a mirror

Just a clock

That allows me enough time to analyze these women

Leaving not a second to look at my self

Call Her Sunshine

I pray you find a distraction soon

Hope she fucks on the first date

Hope her pussy smells like lavender

She studies contortionism and

Has a relaxed gag reflex

Let her come with

Whatever it takes to keep you off my missed calls list

Stop texting me "I miss you"

You don't miss me yet

You won't even be aware of how to miss me until

She cooks you breakfast in bed

(Or she doesn't cook
you breakfast in bed)
And every bite is
missing that creole
spice

Until you try to discuss racial injustice with her

And her flame doesn't set fire to your soul

Until yo' mama asks if I'm doing alright

And all you can say is "I hope so"

'Cuz you won't know

I will not linger

(Not physically)

However

My absence is more of a theory than an absolute

I took all my shoes and pictures

To make room for your contemplation and her suspicions

Practice keeping your face straight when she asks if you still think about me

Tell her no

Tell yourself no

(Tell yourself again)

Convince yourself

Use your words for something other than polluting my voicemail Hover yo' cloud elsewhere

Stop calling me yo' ex

In fact from now on, call me the umbrella

You appreciated during thunderstorms

But didn't have the sense to use for shade

Even after I told you I missed the sun

I'm sure your distraction will arrive in the summer

You'll cool her with fair weather promises

You'll learn to use your lost love ballads as lullabies

You won't miss me

Truly miss me

Until it rains and all she can offer you are warm wishes

Magic

I stopped believing in magic at 30

Seemed like a good time, if any

I stopped believing shortly after you asked

"Do you realize how much you cost me?"

Even if I could forget that I was born broke

That poverty is only a failed relationship away

That my pretty
helps me eat
You wouldn't
let me

I should've went corporate, like you

Made my life all numbers and after work happy hours

Ain't a lot of happy hours in nonprofit

(Captain Obvious would tell you ain't a lot of profit either)

Some weeks I make more CPS reports than I make love

Ain't no magic here

Just grant deficiency and lovers who hate

Who remind you "you ain't that fucking smart"

Like I didn't tell myself that same affirmation this morning

I've stopped believing in magic

While I'm at it, fairy tales too

In fact fairy tales are the fucking worst

They combine magic and human decency

(If even one of those things actually existed

They'd never flow into the same room and

Wrap their arms around one lucky girl)

    And I'll tell you something else

    Cinderella was a fucking junkie

    Ain't have no pumpkin coach either

    Most likely found a pill man named Prince

    Got so high she broke her ankle and swore her shoe fell off

If your daughter is any shade of brown

Any hue of urban

Any complexion of broke

Stop reading her fairy tales

Never take her to a magic show

So on days she ain't got 2 nickels to rub together

She won't waste time looking behind her ears for quarters

Looking up the street for prince charming

Looking in the mirror for any fair anything that falls in her favor

'Cause even when it seems things are falling in her favor

She manages a come up

She marries up

She holds her hand out for 4 carats instead of a hand out

There be an evil witch passing her apples

That smell like stability

Look like longevity

Taste like love

The apple never tastes
like poison, does it
(Does it)

Maybe when you grow up hungry

Anything you eat tastes like love

Smells like happily ever after

Looks like a big fucking apple

I am done with fairy tales

I don't know how much I cost you

Your tone tells me I wasn't worth it

Candle Thrower –a short

I know that you are going to tell your new girlfriend about that time I threw a lit candle at the wall

I wish you'd include some context

I dare to dream you'd admit some fault

But I've been a new girlfriend enough times to know

Back stories and details are quickly forgotten in the arms of new lovers

I've been a new girlfriend enough times to know

That both you and her

Need me to be a crazy, candle tossing lady

So go 'head

Tell her

GET OFF'A ME (and other shit I yelled in fights)

Forgiveness

Maybe I have a little

Just a pinch of forgiveness stored up

A few leftover
seeds from my
mother My
father

Not enough to plant a tree worth anything

But a seed or two Enough

I keep them on the top shelf

I keep the step ladder in the basement

I can't convince my feet you are worth the trouble

But if the shelf ever falls

If gravity

Old age

And the weight of a few seeds

Ever pull the shelf down

I'll plant you a houseplant

When the leaves are big enough I'll bring it to you

Give you a second chance to play God

To honor or neglect a living thing

To decide a forever

To sow more seeds

Make amends in a way

That means more than your apologies ever will

> ***I don't know what you were trying to beat out of me so I'll never know if you succeeded.***

Push came to shove, shove came to slap, open-hand slaps became closed-fist punches, and mall trips became trips to the emergency room.

I met her at Stacy's. Not my favorite place in the world, but my homegirls were there and it was Ladies Night. I don't consider myself a night club regular but it is a safe way to meet other lesbians. (We know that dating is hard. Even harder when you are a part of an isolated, often closeted subculture.) Anyway, I found myself in one of those dark, cheaply-decorated, overpriced-drink-serving, drag-show-hosting, gay bars. She was at our table with my homegirl, Tammi; they patronized the same weed man— which in the hood basically made them cousins. She asked if she could buy me a drink. I told her I didn't drink. She responded, "I'm not much of a drinker either." When I eyeballed her drink she raised her glass and said, "But when in Rome . . ."

We found a semi-quiet spot and talked for at least an hour. She asked me about my interests; I mentioned my one-year-old son. To my delight, she told me she was a kindergarten music and art teacher. (She was always what the situation called for.) We left the club together that night. I thought we were going to have sex but the second her head hit the pillow, she was out.

Outside of bathroom breaks and food, she didn't leave my bed for three days. During that time we talked A LOT. I wasn't working and she wasn't teaching summer classes, so we spent our time getting to know one another. We exchanged life stories. She'd suffered unspeakable abuse and pain growing up. After hearing about her childhood I felt an overwhelming desire to protect her. On the fourth day she had to go out of town for a job-related conference. While she was away I received a package that contained diapers and toys for my son and a bracelet for me. I'd known her less than a week . . . About six job-related conferences later the questions started to pile up:

> *Why did she need to go out of town so often?*
> *Why didn't she ever have a normal work schedule? Why'd she always have so much cash on hand?*

She never answered these questions. She didn't have to.

So shopping, shopping, shopping. We shopped. When things were good, to celebrate. When things were bad, as a distraction. I suppose I was happy—but not really. I looked up and realized I had spent over a year in the mall. I was bored. I had nothing to fill my days. I didn't work or go to school because she needed me on-call in case she needed bail money or an alibi, and "job money" came too slow. I couldn't socialize with too many people because I didn't want my lifestyle, combined with my lack of job, questioned. My son was in daycare five days a week. The highlight of my day was getting him dressed and taking him to daycare. That was my only reason to leave the house most days. I wanted him to socialize with other kids, but I also wanted to decrease the chances of him being home in the likely event police showed up with a warrant.

I was in a relationship with a person who was able to lie, scheme, and fraud enough to financially support herself, me, my son, and many of her family members. BUT I expected her to be honest and genuine with *me*. The good thing about being naïve is it eventually wears off. I was only slightly shocked when her boyfriend showed up at my door.

She was a liar. Sometimes to my benefit, sometimes to my heartache, but always a liar. I knew she was under a tremendous amount of pressure. She had to avoid being caught by the police when earning a living. She had to avoid being caught by her girlfriend while cheating. After a year or so the stress from all that pressure started to manifest itself into fist fights. In the two years before I left, I learned that a purplebased smoky eye covers a black eye better than concealer. I learned that a threeyear-old and emergency room staff look at you the same way when you say, "I'm really leaving this time." I learned that abuse is not homophobic. Abuse will show up in your gay, trans, queer, gender non-conforming, hetero, poly-, bi relationship and kick yo' ass. "It won't happen again" is the truest statement my ex ever spoke. It never happens again—quite the same way. It built up as I broke down. It grew as I shrunk. It was different each time. So was I. It always happened, but never again like the time before.

Loud

I tried to listen to your half ass apologies but

You mouth swells with broken promises

Your breath smells like lies brewing

My ears are smaller than my heart

Smarter than my heart

Accept less bullshit

This isn't what either of us had in mind

This is what happens after months of miscommunication

Countless
bruisesthe *It
won't happen
again* Plays in
my head
before you
even say it

This is the kind of silence that only follows screams

Its gets harder to forgive each time

That it doesn't happen again

Like the last time and the time before that

Even harder to smile through your own blood

In family photos

On make-up dates

I'll shut up

This only happens because I forget to

Watch my fucking mouth
I'll buy a camcorder

Install it in my gums

Surveillance my words

And trap the ones that trigger blows behind my teeth

But something tells me

You'll still find a reason

I've run out of places to put the Band-Aids

The

New-purse-paid-bill-long-stem-roses Band-Aids

There are no words worth speaking

I ain't listening to yours

I'm afraid of my own

Silence makes no promises

Yells no pleas

I love the
sounds we
don't make
Fair Fight

They'll say it directly to you

While your bruises are in various stages of healing

Side-eye you when you say "girlfriend"

Name of the ways and reasons they'd never stay after the first time

Never allow another woman
to push them down Never be
you

I can almost guarantee you the first time you've felt fingers that have brought you pleasure

Palms that have kissed your own

Reconfigure themselves into a grenade
landing on your head Gender will not be
important

It won't even be about strength

It will be about pain

And your bruises will be the least of it

I wish I could tell you or myself

I wouldn't let another person hit me

I would just fight back

But my reactions aren't hypothetical

They are documented

By Henry Ford's emergency room

But even more telling

In the eyes of my son

Who was 2 when I watched him use superman to beat Barbie's ass

Because *Mommy, his girlfriend won't shut up*

I wish I could tell you I don't know why he did that

Or that I didn't listen when she said

Get up, bitch. Quit acting like I hurt you. You want to leave?
Go 'head, ain't nobody gon' want cho ass anyway
I want to tell you I've never used tear-soaked checks to pay daycare fees

I've never worn a long sleeve shirt in a heat wave

I cain't tell you much about never

I can tell you what it feels like to ask your sister if she'd take care of your son

If you were no longer around

I can tell you how bad the charcoal
used to induce vomiting taste I can tell
you when the EMS tech ask you *How*
many pills did you take?

Not enough, isn't the right answer

When your abuser is also your emergency contact

It won't feel like a fair fight

And maybe she's right

Maybe I'm more drama queen than victim

And you, random girl who overheard my situation

In a hospital waiting room

Maybe you are right

And I should count my blessings

These W*ell, at least it ain't no man* blessings
My fair fight blessings

Leaving

You are free to watch me pack, but I'm going to ask that you do so quietly

That conflict resolution shit we learned in therapy is escaping me right now

Don't do it

Don't ask me why I'm leaving

Why the fuck is leaving always questioned anyway

When the real issue is usually staying

Stayed way to long for my leaving to be questioned

You watched me regurgitate my soul

Bite into it for nourishment

Swallow chunks, push it out

And snack on the feces

But never acknowledged the shit

Don't move your lips to
accuse me of giving up
How the fuck can I give
what I don't have?

I ain't had no UP in 3 years

Plenty of DOWN though

Down to spare

ANYBODY NEED SOME DOWN

You act like packing is the beginning of some sad story

Packing is the credits

The applause that happens after the second encore

Packing is clearing the table

It is sunset, it is midnight

It is not the beginning of anything

You insult me with your disbelief

Your shock says you'd thought I'd stay

Fix yo' face

Look at me with less surprise

Look at me like you saw this coming

Like you've been mentally preparing for this for months

Like you view me as a fully capable woman

Who is smart enough to stop banging her head against a rock Because it's in a pillowcase

Don't ask me why I'm leaving

Ask me something relevant

Ask me who gets the casserole dish we bought together Is it mine or yours

Maybe I'll just take the bottom, leave you the lid

Show you how it feels to have something that only works When the other half is present

My absence is a response to your abandonment

We needn't speak at all

But understand

If a woman cries and no one is around to catch the tears

They still make a sound Even in

silence

When you turn your pillow over

Be aware that a rainstorm happened there

Know that I was polite enough to clear out the debris

But the water damage,

The water damage don't clean up so easy

I'll leave you with yours

And pack mine in my already overflowing baggage

Better to Have Loved

Spoons

I kept this spoon

It's the only thing of yours that I didn't

Return

Donate

Burn

Destroy

From our time together

I keep it on a shelf

High up

Never use it

Not because it's yours

Not because it touched your mouth

(Therefore making it some invaluable relic)

But because you didn't even notice it was gone

It reminds me that things don't cease to exist

Don't change form

Nor lose significance once it is no longer yours

If the spoon is still here, then so am I

"tis better to have loved and lost than to never have loved at all" -Lord Tennyson

I've repeated this quote in an effort to bullshit myself at least 10,000 times.

I fell in love once. It was the kind of experience that will forever have me question which is greater: the experience or the aftermath? I lived in the experience for a moment. I have lived in the aftermath forevermore.

This lover I remember in seasons. We met in the spring. It was a wet, soggy spring that threatened to hold summer hostage. We kept dry by going to cafes and restaurants. Everything I ordered was amazing that spring . . .

Summer didn't announce itself that year. It showed up quiet but raging hot. Maybe I didn't notice because I'd been so warm, inside all spring. That year, summer served merely as an excuse to undress. We basked in that excuse. Often.

We spilled into fall—dipping between infatuation and love. We leaned toward love, tipped the scales, then fell in. It was fall when I learned her grandmother's recipe for pound cake. Fall, when I got to spend the wealth of her bookshelf. Fall, when we had our first argument. (As much as I've tried, I can't remember what it was about. I know that I was loud and passionate about it. I know that I was right.) I learned how gently and mindfully she reacted to loud, passionate black women. Fall was still and affirming; so was she.

As always, invited or not, winter came. That winter was mild in temperature but heavy with snow. Not important, but it's what I see when I close my eyes. Snow covering cars and rooftops. Her sixth-floor apartment, with all the downtown

Detroit charm you could fit in one building, had quite a view. That apartment was so damn Detroit that the heat was controlled by management. There was always so much steam. From the radiators. And from us.

The last time we made love, there was so much steam, I slipped on my way to open the window; she was kind enough to pretend not to see. When I finally got this old, screen-less, half-painted window open, I smelled the snow. In that moment, so clear, I learned that snow has a scent.

That beautiful winter passed. Winter always takes something with it though, doesn't it? As mild as that winter was, every flowerbed and tree limb survived. I guess we were the sacrifice.

Weeping Willow

You were a willow tree

Standing tall, while reaching

Arms always extended, giving

Claimed your reward was in my smile

I laughed but didn't believe you

(I believed you when you showed me more than you told me)

I felt like this one time before

I was 7

It was my first time on the giant slide

The rug slipped from under me

I spent 15 seconds (that felt like 2 hours) reaching for it

It was the only thing that mattered in that moment

Exhilarating, scary, free . . . so free

Now you should understand that for black girls,

For black women attempting to

Love, forgive, pray away systemic post slavery shackles

Free be better than pretty

Better than rich,
better than full
Free be the only
thing worth risking
it all for

And love, didn't we risk it all?

We must have

Because it's all gone now

I felt you pull your roots out

Sometimes I trip in the hole you left

Now I'm the only thing weeping here

Any Memories

Do you remember me fondly

Tell me, past lover

Does my name dance on the pages of
your journal Adagio-style across the
pages

Do I monopolize 10—no 20 pages of your auto-biography

Did I love you enough for 20 pages

Do you write of our
experiences in
cursive Am I a haiku
yet

Do you still have my cards, past lover

Do you use them as bookmarks

Have they maybe filled a shoebox

Please tell me you didn't put them in the compost

Do you still garden

Make beautiful things bloom amongst shit and concrete?

Place flowers where they wouldn't be

Are you still growing, my love

What parts did you save

Any good, any smiling, any forever parts

Am I still there

With you, on train rides, and in cafes

Do wildflowers remind you of my perfume

Reminding you of wildflowers

Do you know I miss you, past lover

I miss you so
deep into the
night that I
miss you into
the morning

Sometimes I get sick from missing you

Sometimes I get well from the experience

Sometimes I get lost in all of it

I believe it's called a memory

Tell me, past lover Am I at least a

memory?

The Native

I see you on every corner

Your eyes had the skyline in 'em

Your arms were Whitney St

Your hands were Linwood Ave

When you held me I was home

You knew the freeways

Backways

And always how to get me there

You knew this city

Like I knew this city

We love this city

Enjoyed too much of it together

So now that I don't see you it's an eyesore

I need to ask you how you

Feel about Midtown

The train

The murals

Or maybe I just want to hear you agree with me

There are seven Coney Islands

Three museums

Two thrift stores

And one very secluded spot on Belle Isle

I can't visit anymore

Probably would get lost anyway

Even if I found it

Who would tell me where to watch my step

I'm loving out-of-towners from now on

From cities where I didn't learn to Double-Dutch

With unfamiliar area codes And

less one-way streets

Cities I don't call home

So it hurts less when lovers don't call at all

Your Books

It is mid-April when I realize

I will never again sit on your couch

And welcome you interrupting me

Reading one of your books

I'll never finish any of the 5 books

I started

Bookmarked

And put back on the shelf

Never borrowed them

I was always coming back Until I wasn't

I took your bookshelf for granted

Treated it like it owed itself to me

Touched its treasure at my leisure

Like there was no rush

As if the pages would never yellow

Had I opened just one

Concentrated

Offered that one its due time

I may have finished it

Might have learned something

Maybe left more than a bookmark

I miss your...bookshelf

Wonder how it's holding up

Have you dusted the corner where the ashes fall

Finally organized them by favorite author

Is someone there

Turning the pages

Moving my bookmarks

Discarding my bookmarks

Helping you forget I left any marks at all

Maybe it's better that I don't know

How egotistical of me to break the bindings and toss the covers

Then wonder if who's turning the pages

Is an avid reader

Did I expect no one to take interest in my absence

Did I believe no woman would desire more than just a preface

I'm no fool

I know your books are in better hands by now

By better I mean

Consistent

Hands capable of forever

I never found the courage to tell you

How regret-ridden

And apologetic

I am

For how I left . . . your bookshelf

Again With the Memories

I've stopped trying to get over missing you

I've learned to accept this emptiness as part of my existence

Matter-of-fact, I'm going to use you for daydreaming

For reminiscing

For checking out

I tried to bury your memories

They dug themselves out

Again and again

(And again and again)

I should've just planted rose bushes

Let them dance

And be free

Enjoy them, those memories

From here on out

You're going to soothe me to sleep

Gon' play in my head when peace avoids me

Our memories will hold my hand

On long days

At dentist appointments

When my mind visits dark places

No use cuddling regret

When memories want to dance

Barefoot and undone

Memories just want space and light and air

Thinking 'bout

How not to think about you

Brings me right back around To

thinking 'bout you

I'm going to give our memories

The same thing I gave you

Space

Silence

Permission to wander

And maybe one day

Like you

They'll just leave me be

LATRODECTUS HESPERUS

Time Again

It's Thursday 2:57 in the afternoon

You are at work

You've had lunch by now

At least one irritating customer and a coffee

It's Friday 9:45 pm You are at the
bar

At 8:pm you said you'd be home by 11:pm

You'll be drunk by 10:15

Which is when 11:pm becomes 2:30

When I'll hear your keys fumbling, dropping

You stumbling

There is a 50/50 chance

You'll make it up the stairs

A 50/50 chance

I'll find you somewhere between the couch and the bathroom tomorrow A 100% chance that I won't care

10:am I've decided you've slept long enough

I vacuum around your head

You get up

Disappear in the bathroom for an hour

It's 11:am Wednesday

You are dropping our youngest off at daycare

You'll call at 11:07 and tell me he cried

I'll remind you to bring home juice

We are always running out of something

We are both home by 9:pm

Found a reason to argue by 9:16

In bed at 10:30

It is here that I lose you

That I have no clue as to where you are

What you feeling

It's here that I don't know how to

What I'm running low on What

we've run out of

At some point my eyes close

My alarm goes off

We wake up

We do it again And again

And again . . .

Whoever said, "It is better to have loved and lost than to have never loved at all," never had to pay alimony.

As I write this, my wife and I are contemplating divorce. Sometimes we discuss it in hushed tones in hopes that it won't hear us. That we won't beckon it and remind each other that it is an option—not a beautiful one, but an option just the same. Sometimes we yell it at each other. Loudly. Louder than when we said our vows. Louder than my screams when I bore our son. Louder still. Louder than all the music in all the bars she frequents in an attempt to escape me. Sometimes we don't say it at all. We just make room for it in our silence. She checks the calendar: Friday looks like a good day for filing paper work. I keep a brand-new pen in my purse—ready. Set. GO . . . GET THE PAPERS!!!

Whole conversations also happen in the silence.

>She says, "Hey, have you seen the remote?"
>
>*She thinks, She's always moving shit. Wish she'd fucking move.*
>
>*I think, Wish I ain't seen yo ass.,*
>
>I say "Nope, I ain't the remote's keeper . . ."
>
>*She thinks, But you are a keeper of secrets. Bitch, I ain't forgot . . .*
>
>She says, "Ok, I'm going to watch the game at the bar."
>
>*I think, Drunky McDrunkerson is headed to the bar again—breaking news.*
>
>I say, "You might wanna get something to eat while you out."
>
>She says, "Okay, you want me to bring you something?" *She thinks,*

I hope she ain't here when I get back.

I say, "No, I'll be fine."

I think, "I'm cooking—just not for you."

Relationships phase out or change organically as we move through life. For instance, when we are born we are fully dependent on our parents (or caregivers). Over time we need them less and less. We leave their home. They enjoy life without a child. The dependent/caregiver relationship naturally concludes, and everyone is better for it. Another relationship is with a teacher. When the class ends, so does your relationship. We know this in the beginning and we accept this in the end. The relationship has a prescribed time. But marriage ain't supposed to end. How do we end what ain't supposed to? Divorce can be worse than death. Death happens in an instant. Divorce can creep up on you. It is severely personal. And it always happens too soon. Even when we saw it coming. (Even when a part of us is relieved.) It's sudden and cold.

If I were ever to become a marriage counselor (no worries, not in the plans), I would encourage engaged couples to spend a day sitting in divorce court. After, they should go home and play jury; discuss who was right and who was wrong; decide who deserved what they asked for; etc. I can almost guarantee this will initiate conversations about marriage, roles in the household, responsibilities, co-parenting and finances in a way no blissfully-in-love couple could do on their own. A divorce is more honest than a wedding. You know exactly who you are divorcing. You are only starting to learn who you are marrying.

Park at Sundown

We are about 19 inches apart on this bench

I hate going to the park in the fall

The sunshine combined with his running

Tricks my son into believing it's warm

Sitting still allows me to feel the chill

And, baaabyyy, it's cold out here

I would ask you to hold me for warmth but

This cold feels familiar

Feels like our bed

Our bed

Or the bed we're still sharing

Simply because neither of us had the foresight

 To buy a house with a spare room

And we are only at this stupid-ass park

Because this is what adults with kids do

Take the kid to a park

Attend our mutual friend's dinner party

Live together in silence

Live together because we live together

Because pretending
drains all your energy
Besides who has the time
Who wants the inconvenience?

We have almost paid off you student loans
I am nearly done with my degree
Your mothers sick
I hate packing
The baby is so little
There is never a good time for a divorce

My son stops running

Waves to us on a park bench

More for us than him

Kids always know

Even if they aren't sure about what it is they know

He goes back to running

You look at me

Over the years I've learned

When you fake smile

You show 6 of your top teeth

When you genuinely smile

You show 8 top and 6 bottom

You smile at me now and I only count 6 top teeth

I get up

Chase my son around

Attempt to warm up

Feel some warmth

Perhaps store some of it for later to thaw our bed

My son leads me under the monkey bars

Tells me we're safe here

Your phone rings

I see you
answer
while on the
bench I
count 8 top
teeth and 6
bottom

I sit on the ground under the monkey bars

I feel safe here

My son has
moved on to
the slide
You have
moved on to
. . .

Whoever it is that has you showing 14 teeth

My son is finally ready to go

He walks up to me and says,

"It's cold and I'm ready to leave now"

Just like that

It's cold and I'm ready to leave now

We exit the park

The only honest person sits in the back

We drive off

I mentally repeat

It's cold and I'm ready to leave

It's cold and I'm ready to leave

It's cold and I'm ready to leave

We get home

I look you in yo' eyes and say, "What chu want for dinner"

My Grandma

My grandmother was poor

Luckily, I hadn't met a rich person til' many years after she'd passed So I was able to judge her solely on her character

She taught me how to sew

Well

She gave me some yellow curtains

Purple thread and instructed, "gon somewhere and sat down"

She taught me to teach myself how to sew

Which taught me I know more than I know I know

There are only
things I haven't

done Nothing I
can't do

My grandmother was dark-skinned

I don't remember anyone ever mentioning this to her face

Which is odd

Because when a woman is dark-skinned

Someone always mentions it

Either in insult or compliment

We never just let
dark-skinned women
be But for some
reason folks let her
be

She died long before I'd ever heard

"Pretty for a dark-skin girl" so I just thought she was pretty

I learned to write her name on green lined paper with thick pencils

Wrote it on applications

My first lease

Eldest sons birth certificate

Wrote it in print and in cursive

By the time I met you

I had learned to write her name gracefully

By the time I met you I understood how poor I was

What my brown skin meant

And how walking away with nothing tears at your soul

I'm telling you this so you understand

What I did when I took your name

How much I gave, what I lost, who I left

I hear you when you yell and when you whisper about my nothingness

The nothingness that I am

That I came with

You are so convinced I'll leave with

Did you tell your lawyer 'bout my grandma

'Bout them recipes I never learned

Radios I never grabbed

'Bout leaving with only a name

Then leaving that name

Is he aware that she visits me in daydreams

And demands to know why I gave away the only thing she could afford to leave me

ARE YOU AWARE

Did you think past the vanity

When I agreed to add to your family's legacy by my works

And my son

And the erasure of myself

I gave my grandmothers name away for love

Some silly concept of unconditional love

And now I have yours

If I could

I'd pawn yours for $20 and a pedicure

Tell your lawyer he should negotiate wisely

Like a man battling a ghost

And 4 generations of Browner
women dying silently With
nothing to pass on but a name

See, I'm going to leave my children fine china

The wasteful kind that sits in a cabinet

Never being used

As a reminder to keep some things for yourself

As a receipt of your alimony

As a sacrifice to my grandma

Ol' Girl

Our marriage has an ol' girl

A woman so significant her name takes the air from a room

So we dare not speak it She's just

ol' girl

Ol' girl is fucking magical

She make vows lose value

Calls go unanswered

And last week she emptied a chair at my dinner table every fucking night

You don't say her name

You say I'm tripping

Say you working late

Say you aren't fucking her

(With obvious disappointment)

Yelling you aren't fucking her is less comforting than you think

Because If that's true

You'd rather spend time with a woman who won't fuck you

Then me, a woman who's been fucking you

Me, a woman so desperate to keep you

I lay crucifix style in bed

Praying for the third day

Even if you aren't seduced by my nudity

Maybe my stretch marks will remind you

Of my humanity or your son

But ol' girl so magical

She's your lovely assistant

Convinced you to saw me in half

And you'd love nothing more than to give her a show

It's Over

It's over and I have to get over it

My friends have done their mandatory check-ins

Brunches, movie nights

They've answered at 3:am

Let me cry, uninterrupted

Each friend took a shift

Did their part

They owe me nothing

It's over and I have to get over it

You've used 2 vacation days

To vacation, in yo' bed

In the dark

On a wet pillow

You have to go in tomorrow

Another day would warrant vacation pics

And a story

You have neither

It's over and I have to get over it

You've done every ritual known to woman

Broken soul ties

Cleansed spirit

Offerings made

Sheets burned

I shopped with money I ain't got

For shit I don't need

Finger and toe nails are pink and shiny

Tipped the nail tech

Called it self-care

Called it necessary

Called out a name in the dark

None but the walls heard

They even seemed to yell back

"Girl, it's over and you got to get over it, do you hear me"
It's over and I've got to get over it

Dear Future Lover

Dear New Lover,

Before I undress in front of you for the first time

I need to beg for your kindness

I don't mean fake compliments

I have no use for them

I'll accept your silence as compliment enough

Just don't *Gasp*

Don't clear your throat as a reaction to your shock

Don't attempt a joke

Stretch marks are not tiger stripes

And you've never wanted to be alone in a room with a tiger

Don't compare me to things you wouldn't want to be in a room with While alone in a room with me

Be kind with your eyes

Keep them from wandering too far into my darkness

Be liberal
with your
imagination
But skilled

enough to
hide it

Only you and God need to know

That you mentally replace my image with a supermodel For heaven's sake don't call me her name

Our sexual experiences will always be a threesome

My insecurities, your disappointment, our collective avoidance

Dear New Lover

I really hope you enjoy creole cuisine

And Random art history facts

 I can impress you in kitchens and museums
But never in swimsuits

I just want your expectations to be realistic

I want you to consider how important physical beauty is to you And respond accordingly

Not wanting to make love to a woman

Whose body reminds you of a road you'd complain to the city about

Still makes you a lover

A lover of honesty

A slayer of future resentments

And 1 less scar I'd need to explain

thank you to Alana Gracey for keeping me motivated and focused

to Juwanna Patrice for helping me bring a dream to life

Cover photo credit, Sahir Al-Salam

Dedications
I dedicate this book to every black femme who has ever found herself on the opposite side of joy.

To Marlisa who always love like its the first time
To Nicky who's drive and knowledge of self combine to create a woman of ambition
To BreAnn who taught me to answer only my name no matter what they call me
and
To Bradleigh #MBGITW because....I wish a nigga would

Made in the USA
Monee, IL
12 June 2024